LEADER'S GUIDE

The **40** DAY
Soul Fast

The 40 DAY Soul Fast

Your Journey to Authentic Living

CINDY TRIMM

DESTINY IMAGE® PUBLISHERS, INC.

P.O. Box 310, Shippensburg, PA 17257-0310

"Promoting Inspired Lives."

This book and all other Destiny Image and Destiny Image Fiction books are available at Christian bookstores and distributors worldwide.

For more information on foreign distributors, call
717-532-3040.

Reach us on the Internet: www.destinyimage.com.

ISBN 13 TP: 978-0-7684-0871-3

ISBN 13 Ebook: 978-0-7684-8758-9

For Worldwide Distribution, Printed in the U.S.A.

10 2024

CONTENTS

GROUP LEADER GUIDELINES

Welcome! If you are reading this, then you are about to begin an amazing journey that will not only transform your life, but the world! This is an eight-week study of the life of the soul, the practice of fasting, and the process of living more authentically. We encourage you to travel on this 40-day journey with a small group from your church, organization, or family. You were not created to journey alone! There is power in community. There is strength in numbers. I challenge you to bring at least 4 friends along with you on your own soul-healing journey to authentic living. When you do, you will be setting a new kind of trend; you will be leading a global transformation, and engaging in an unprecedented movement for the good of humanity.

As you begin this journey, this set of guidelines will help you experience the best 40 days of your life, as well as give you the tools to lead others through this journey to authentic living!

STEPS TO STARTING A *40 DAY SOUL FAST* GROUP

CONSIDER THE JOURNEY!

Pray! Ask the Holy Spirit, the "*Spirit of truth,*" as He is called in John 16:13, to give you guidance as you make your plans. This 40-day journey will talk a great deal about resting in your Creator, what that means, and how it can empower you to live more authentically. We are told in Jeremiah, "*Stop at the crossroads and look around. Ask for the old, godly way, and walk in it. Travel its path, and you will find rest for your souls...*" (Jer. 6:16 NLT)

MAP OUT YOUR COURSE!

Determine a meeting location. Keep in mind the number of people who may attend. You will also need audio-visual equipment. The more comfortable the setting, the more people will enjoy being there, and will spend more time ministering to each other! Smaller groups may work well meeting in homes, larger groups may need a church or community center to accommodate them. Just a word of caution here—the larger the group, the greater your need for co-leaders or assistants. The ideal small group is difficult to judge, however once you get more than 10-12 people, it becomes difficult for each member to feel "heard." If your group is larger than 12 people, consider having 2 or more small group discussion leaders. Break out into smaller discussion groups, each led by an assistant.

Determine the format of your Soul Fast meetings. At this point, also determine the extent of your fast. The purpose of the Soul Fast is to eliminate toxins in your soul, *not* your body. However, because the soul and body are interconnected, what is good for one is good for the other! We encourage you to take this opportunity to cleanse and detox your body as you dedicate yourself to cleansing and detoxifying your soul. If you choose to pursue a physical fast along with the soul fast, please read Appendix A: *The 40 Day Soul Fast Handbook*. Prior to any type of physical fasting, individuals should consult with their doctor.

Once you have established the extent of your fast, set a schedule for your meetings. Some groups like to have a time of fellowship or socializing either before or after the teaching time, where light refreshments are offered. If you are also pursuing a physical fast—be mindful of the foods that your group members may be fasting from! Water flavored with slices of lemon, lime and/or orange, fresh fruit or vegetable juices, as well as herbal and green teas are all good choices, as well as fruit or vegetable trays with hummus or yogurt dips. Be careful not to focus on food however—always keep in mind the purpose is to focus on healing your soul!

Establish a start date along with a weekly meeting day and time. This eight-week course should be followed consistently and consecutively. Be mindful of the fact that while there are eight weeks of material, most groups will want to meet one last time after completing the 40th day of work to celebrate. Look far enough ahead on the calendar to account for anything that might interfere. Choose a weeknight, Saturday morning, or Sunday school time at your church depending on the members of your group.

Advertise! Getting the word out in multiple ways is most effective. Print up flyers, post a sign-up sheet, make announcement in church services or group meetings, set up your own blog or website or post the event on the social media avenue you and your group utilize. A personal invitation is a great way to reach those who might need that little bit of extra encouragement.

Gather your materials. Each leader will need the *40 Day Soul Fast DVD Study* (which comes with the leader's guide), *The 40 Day Soul Fast* study guide as well as *The 40 Day Soul Fast* book. Additionally, each participant will need a personal copy of both the *40 Day Soul Fast* book and *study guide*. We have found it best for the materials to all be purchased at one time–many booksellers offer discounts on multiple orders, and you are assured that each member will have their materials from the beginning.

STEP FORWARD!

Arrive at your meeting in *plenty* of time to prepare; frazzled last minute preparations do not put you in a place of "rest," and your group member will sense your stress! Ensure that all A/V equipment is working properly, and that you have ample supplies for each member. Nametags are a great idea, at least for the first couple of meetings. Icebreaker and introduction activities are also a good idea for the first meeting.

Pray for your members. As much as possible, make yourself available to them. As each person discovers their authentic self, they will want to share that discovery! You will also need to encourage those who struggle, grow weary, or lose heart. Make sure your members stay committed so they experience the full benefits of soul healing.

Embrace the transformational journey that you and your fellow members are embarking on to authentic living! Transformation begins within *you!*

Multiply yourself. Is there someone you know who was not able to attend your group? Help them to initiate their own small group now that you know how effective soul cleansing can be in a group setting!

Thank you for doing your part in creating a global movement! By helping to heal the world one soul at a time–you are impacting culture with God's greatest good.

It's a better world because of you!

GROUP LEADER CHECKLIST

1–2 Months Prior

__ Have you determined a start date?

__ Have you determined the format, meeting day and time, and weekly meeting schedule?

___ Have you selected a meeting location (making sure you have adequate space and A/V equipment available)?

___ Have you advertised? Do you have a sign-up sheet to ensure you order enough materials?

2 Weeks–1 Month Prior

___ Have your ordered materials? You will need a copy of *The 40 Day Soul Fast* and the Participants Guide for each participant.

___ Have you organized your meeting schedule/format?

1–2 Weeks Prior

___ Have you received all your materials?

___ Have you reviewed the DVD's and your Leader's Guide to familiarize yourself with the material, and to ensure everything is in order?

___ Have you planned and organized your refreshments, if you are planning to provide them? Some leaders will handle this themselves, and some leaders find it easier to allow participants to sign up to provide refreshments if they would like to do so.

First Meeting Day

Plan to arrive *early!* Give yourself extra time to set up the meeting space, double check all A/V equipment and organize your materials. It might be helpful to ask participants to arrive 15 minutes early the first meeting to allow for distribution of materials and any ice-breaker activity you might have planned.

INTRODUCTION

*It is my own firm belief that the strength of the
soul grows in proportion as you subdue the flesh.*
—MOHANDAS GANDHI

*Is not this the kind of fasting I have chosen: to
loose the chains of injustice and untie the cords
of the yoke, to set the oppressed free and break
every yoke?*
—ISAIAH 58:6 NIV

Welcome to *The 40 Day Soul Fast Leader's Guide!* The
volume you hold in your hand will accompany you on
this eight-week journey. I am on a mission to reconnect you with the true essence of a healthy soul—to
lead you to a place in God where your soul can be
healed—to reacquaint you with your authentic self.
The next 40 days of getting to know the real you
are going to be the best 40 days of your life! More
importantly, when you learn to live authentically,
from a healed, whole soul, no leaks, no punctures, no

wounds—free and clear from artificial, socially modi-
fied, cultural toxins—you will not only change your
life, you will be poised to change the world.

We have all heard the phrases, "She's a beautiful
soul," "Bless your soul," or "He's a mean old soul."
These phrases describe our perception of an individual's nature or character. We are all "soul-people,"
and I believe that strengthening people at the level
of their souls—restoring the soul and establishing
it as the core and essence of who they really are as
self-directed people of value, intelligence, and great-
ness—will change the world. We must break the false
perception that as individuals, what we do does not
make a difference in the greater scheme of things. We
are as a nation, as a people, nothing more than the
sum of our parts. As the giant world-changer, a small
man by the name of Mohandas Gandhi, once said, "A
nation's culture resides in the hearts and in the soul
of its people." We will only be as whole and healed
as a country as we are as a people. Oscar Wilde, the
famous Irish poet and novelist said, *"Ordinary riches
can be stolen, real riches cannot. In your soul are infinitely
precious things that cannot be taken from you."* To reiter-
ate a soul-searching question posed by Jesus, "What
does it really profit us if we gain the whole world and

lose our souls—the essence of who we really are and what it means to be human?"

If you are here reading this today, I imagine you have asked yourself that same question. For those of you looking to reclaim your soul and recapture the essence of who you really are, you are in the right place. I created this 40-Day Guide to guide you step-by-step, day-by-day, into a more authentic life. I am so glad you have chosen to join me on this journey to greater mental, emotional, and spiritual health! If you are looking to transform your life, you need look no further! Let the journey begin!

WHAT IS A SOUL FAST?

The purpose of this *40 Day Soul Fast* is to not only bring health and restoration to the souls of individuals, but also to provide a mechanism for all people to learn to live from the inside out—from their authentic, God-nature selves. This Soul Fast is not addressing the issue of what you are eating, but what's eating you. The goal of this 40-day journey is to guide you through the process of discarding useless toxic emotions—self-sabotaging thoughts and viruses of the mind—so that you can fully move into who God created you to be. You will be invited to examine all of your objectives and relationships, any hidden agendas or motives that have governed your subconscious, in order to thrust you onto a new path of achievement and abundance. This journey is about setting you free once and for all to maximize your greatest potential.

The 40-Day Soul Fast takes place over eight weeks. For simplicity's sake, I have taken these eight weeks and divided them evenly so that participants can establish a regular routine Monday through Friday, allowing for weekends off so those going through the study guide can focus on family and worship or make up a missed day if necessary. Encourage your group/class to engage the daily exercises in the study guide, as the more they invest into the study, the more they will benefit from it.

As you lead and facilitate the *40 Day Soul Fast* study, be mindful of the following:

Promote participation in the daily exercises. It's not enough for people to simply attend a session once a week; the study guide is designed to help each participant reinforce the invaluable principles they are learning and interact with them in a very personal way.

Encourage participants to put aside time for "me-moments." Invite group members to give themselves adequate time to focus on nurturing their inner selves. Part of the soul fast discipline is not allowing everyday distractions to deter participants from cultivating the inner life of the soul. It will require disciplined focus, a heightened mindfulness, and keen sensitivity to the Spirit of God.

We will begin our 40-day journey by talking about capacity building. Week one of our eight-week venture focuses on "The Power of 40: Enlarging Your

Capacity." This theme is more fully explored in *The 40 Day Soul Fast,* but for the purposes of this manual, it ties together the five characteristics you will find in week one. In week two, we will talk about "The Purpose of a Soul Fast: The Self-Leadership Challenge." In week three, we will discuss "The Nature of the Soul: The Essence of You." In week four, we address "The Properties of Thought: You Are What You Think." Week five brings us to "The Importance of Identity: Becoming a Master by Mastering Your Mind." In week six we look at "The Power of Words: Healing the Hole in Your Soul." In week seven, we begin wrapping up by dealing with "The Power of Doing: God's Chosen Fast." And in week eight, we conclude by "Sealing the Healing: The Cleansing Power of Love."

The focus of this study is developing the 40 characteristics of an authentic person. These characteristics tie in with *The 40 Day Soul Fast,* but you can also use this curriculum by itself as a tool for focused self-exploration.

Each day, participants will read a meditation about one of the 40 characteristics of an authentic person. Then they will be given several "Action Steps" to consider as they put these characteristics into practice. Encourage group members to fully engage in the study, using the space provided in their study guides to write their responses, reflections, meditations, and anything else God places on their hearts as they delve into these powerful characteristics of authenticity.

THE SOUL OF THE MATTER

> Be your authentic self. Your authentic self is who you are when you have no fear of judgment or before the world starts pushing you around and telling you who you're supposed to be. Your fictional self is who you are when you have a social mask on to please everyone else. Give yourself permission to be your authentic self.
>
> —DR. PHIL MCGRAW

This *40 Day Soul Fast* is about finding rest and restoration for the soul. When all is well with the souls of humanity, all will be well in the world. When people have peace in their souls, they will bring that peace to bear on the world around them—people will become the change they are hoping to see.

Over the next eight weeks, you will learn and grow and be empowered like never before to maximize your personal potential and break through to greater success.

May we all feel the presence of God each and every day as we *"do our best to enter that rest"* (Heb. 4:11 NLT). And as we take up residence there, may we become more acquainted with our authentic selves and equipped to walk in the light of what we discover.

Encourage participants to let their study guides become tools they can use to clear the ground of every obstruction and build lives of obedience into full maturity—the fully complete soul!

Are you ready to begin the best 40 days of your life?

Let the soul journey begin!

> *Beloved, I pray that you may prosper in all things and be in health, just as your soul prospers* (3 John 1:2 NKJV).

You don't have a soul. You are a Soul.
> —C. S. LEWIS

Week One

THE POWER OF 40: ENLARGING YOUR CAPACITY

Pray! Ask God to direct each person to the goal that He has for them as they step out into this journey, and for the wisdom to lead.

WELCOME AND INTRODUCTIONS
(15-30 MINUTES)

- Introduce yourself, and allow each participant to briefly introduce themselves and share their reason for joining this journey.

- Discuss the schedule for the meetings, as well as the entire 40 day journey.

- Distribute materials to each participant. Briefly orient the participants to the book and participants guide, explaining the time commitment for each day. Encourage each person to engage fully in this journey–they will get out of it only as much as they invest.

- Go over Appendix A in the Leaders Guide/Participants Guide. If you or your participants will be doing a physical fast in addition to the Soul Fast, please take time to go over the guidelines. Answer questions as you feel comfortable–always encourage your participants to get the approval of their physician before beginning a physical fast.

VIDEO/TEACHING (30 MINUTES)

DRILLING DOWN (30 MINUTES)

- Review the weekly plan as discussed in the video–5 days of journal entries, weekends off.

- Ask your participants to identify a goal or prayer request–they may share if comfortable. At this point, also discuss trust, confidentiality and transparency with your group. Members will need to know that they are in a safe environment–no one will discuss any detail of your discussions outside the meeting times. This will allow members to share more openly.

- Take a good look at your life, environment, habits and relationships. What are the things that move you closer to your best life? Farther away?

- What do you sense is keeping you from maximizing your potential?

- What keeps you from living more freely and authentically?

- Point out the 24 questions on page 68 of the book and page 161 in the study guide. Encourage participants to answer these questions as they are able.

JOURNEY PLANS FOR THE NEXT WEEK

Point out Day 1–Day 5 in the book and guide. Encourage everyone to participate fully in this journey in order to get the most out of it.

CLOSE IN PRAYER

VIDEO LISTENING GUIDE

Could things be the way they are because you are the way you are?

What one thing could you change that could change everything?

Living authentically means living <u>inside out</u>, not <u>outside in.</u>

Everything you need to succeed at life was given to you at <u>conception.</u>

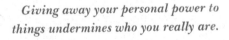

Giving away your personal power to things undermines who you really are.

It's not about what you're eating, but what's eating you.

40 Day Soul Fast is about <u>resting</u> in who <u>God</u> says you are.

Your soul houses your <u>mind, will, emotions.</u>

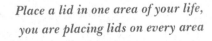

Place a lid in one area of your life, you are placing lids on every area

There are no limitations except <u>the limitations in your mind.</u>

You will place a lid on your own life as long as you think it is someone else's responsibility to make you happy or successful.

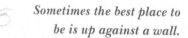

Sometimes the best place to be is up against a wall.

History is going to be kind to me for I intend to write it.

—WINSTON CHURCHILL

You will resemble those with whom you assemble.

<u>Enabling</u> a person is not the same thing as <u>empowering</u> a person.

Everything we want in life lies just <u>beyond</u> our <u>comfort zone.</u>

Capacity building starts with someone challenging you, or you challenging yourself.

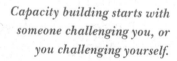

What limitation are you going to remove? Be specific! Dr. Trimm used the term "self imposed impotence." Where is the source of that lie?

Week Two

THE PURPOSE OF A SOUL FAST: THE SELF-LEADERSHIP CHALLENGE

Pray! Ask Holy Spirit for guidance and wisdom as you seek to understand the purpose of a Soul Fast.

STEP OUT ON THE JOURNEY (15 MINUTES)

Review the first week. Encourage members to share observations, comments or ask questions.

VIDEO/TEACHING (30 MINUTES)

DRILLING DOWN (30 MINUTES)

- What are the major events or decisions—or lack thereof—that brought you to where you are now? What is the fruit (rotting, perhaps!) you are carrying with you as a result? Be sensitive to areas of regret or shame that may surface.

- What have you chosen to believe about yourself and others? How is that reflected in your relationships?

- Think on this: the speed at which you choose to believe a thought is how quickly you change the course of your destiny. Your life is simply a representation of the sum total of your choices, choices that either enslave or save your soul. Ultimately, you are only one decision away from changing everything! How does this make you feel? Encouraged?

- Purpose to do this–from here forward, make the decision to align everything you say or do with the Word of God. What do you think will change as a result of this one decision?

JOURNEY PLANS FOR THE NEXT WEEK

Point out Day 6–Day 10 in the book and guide. Encourage everyone to participate fully in this journey in order to get the most out of it.

CLOSE WITH PRAYER

VIDEO LISTENING GUIDE

Heal the soul—heal <u>families</u>, <u>communities</u>, <u>governments</u>.

We seek God's face not just to hear Him talk about <u>Himself</u>, but so that we can hear Him talk about <u>us!</u>

The more you know about <u>God</u>, the more you know about <u>yourself.</u>

What you focus on fuels your <u>thoughts</u>, and whatever fuels your thoughts determines your <u>future</u>.

Not only about fasting, it's about feasting

Connecting for capacity is not just the capacity for where we're going, but to embrace and love where we came from, because that's why we are the way we are.

You cannot impact people and be the leader you should be if you cannot lead <u>yourself</u>.

What's your skeleton? What do you need to pronounce a benediction on?

In being you will do, but in doing you won't have the capacity to be.

What scaffolding are you using to prop up your life?

No matter how good or bad a situation, to give something up there is a grieving process.

There is only one part of this universe that you can guarantee changing, and that's <u>yourself</u>.

Wholeness requires you to <u>accept</u> <u>responsibility</u> for what you choose to let <u>inhabit your heart.</u>

You are only one decision away from being where you want to be!

Where do you want to be?
Who or what have you allowed to steal your peace?

If it's not paying rent—kick it out!

Week Three

THE NATURE OF THE SOUL: THE ESSENCE OF YOU

Pray! Ask Creator God for wisdom as you seek to understand the nature of the Soul.

STEP OUT ON THE JOURNEY (15 MINUTES)

Review the second week. Encourage members to share observations, comments or ask questions.

VIDEO/TEACHING (30 MINUTES)

DRILLING DOWN (30 MINUTES)

- Look up Isaiah 58:6 and Galatians 5:1– have a volunteer read each passage aloud.

- What you allow to govern your soul is what you permit to occupy it. Do you agree with this?

- Is your soul governed by the love of *things*, or the love of God?

- What do you spend the most time thinking about?

- What do you most hope and long for–in general? For this Soul Fast?

- How can you be a child of God and still a slave to sin?

- What are the toxins and ties contaminating and entangling your soul, keeping it vulnerable to sin and cycles of failure?

Journey Plans for the Next Week

Point out Day 11–Day 15 in the book and guide. Encourage everyone to participate fully in this journey in order to get the most out of it.

Close in Prayer

Allow time for personal prayer requests.

VIDEO LISTENING GUIDE

How can you do what you do in such a simple way that the whole world says "that's true elegance"?

> *Is not this the kind of fasting I have chosen: to loose the chains of injustice and untie the cords of the yoke, to set the oppressed free and break every yoke?* (Isaiah 58:6).

> *It is for freedom that Christ has set us free. Stand firm, then, and do not let yourselves be burdened again by a yoke of slavery* (Galatians 5:1).

Your soul can be _____

> *You don't have a soul, you are a soul.*

Nephish (Greek)—<u>breathing</u>, <u>thinking</u>, <u>being</u>, <u>a complete living being</u>.

<u>Spirit</u> makes you God-conscious

<u>Body</u> makes you world-conscious

<u>Soul</u> makes you self-conscious—ability to say
that you are separate from others.

The soul is (lots of answers/space to take notes)

_____

_____

Soul houses <u>mind</u>, <u>will</u>, <u>emotions</u>, <u>seat of your
consciousness</u>, <u>intelligence</u>, <u>reason.</u>

To ignore your soul is to ignore yourself.

You are not the roles that you play.

You cannot turn to the <u>created</u> to determine
who you are, you've got to go to the <u>Creator</u>!

What is unique about you?

Who really knows you, with your mask down?

What's keeping you from finding your unique
expression—that one thing that God
has put you here to do?

What spin has God placed on your humanity that is so
different that you add value to other people?

What really brings you joy?

What are your joy stealers, and how
do you deal with them?

THE PROPERTIES OF THOUGHT: YOU ARE WHAT YOU THINK

Pray! Ask Creator God for wisdom as you seek to understand the thought patterns that rule our Soul.

STEP OUT ON THE JOURNEY (15 MINUTES)

Review the third week. Encourage members to share observations, comments or ask questions.

VIDEO/TEACHING (30 MINUTES)

DRILLING DOWN (30 MINUTES)

- "Winning the battle in your thought life requires daily meditation on the truths found in Scripture, studying the Word of God, and becoming an earnest and life-long student of the art of spiritual warfare." Does this line up with your current belief system? Have you experienced spiritual warfare?

- Every battle is won or lost in the arena of your mind. How can you prepare for these battles? What weapons have we been given? What is your training regimen?

- What are your thoughts on your current 'thoughts'?

- How have you experienced 'thinking for a change'?

- Read Philippians 4:8 aloud! Encourage participants to commit this verse to memory!

Journey Plans for the Next Week

Point out Day 16–Day 20 in the book and journal. Encourage everyone to participate fully in this journey in order to get the most out of it.

Close in Prayer

VIDEO LISTENING GUIDE

*Your thoughts brought you to
where you are today.*

*Whatever things are true, noble, just, pure,
lovely, good report, virtue, praise—think on
these things. And the God of peace [untrou-
bled, undisturbed well-being] will be with you*
(Philippians 4:8-9).

The meaning of a word is always in a <u>person</u>,
and we must take <u>responsibility</u> for how we
interpret it.

Are you prepared to take responsibility for
what goes on in your thought life?

*Why do we make someone else's
reality about us our reality?*

The quality of your <u>thoughts</u> and the quality of
your <u>reality</u> are inextricably related.

> *You learn by experience, but it doesn't have to be your experience!*

Your <u>imagination</u> is more powerful than your <u>memory</u>.

As a man thinks [continues to rehearse over and over] in his heart, so he is (Proverbs 23:7).

Can you be better than what you are now?
What is your life philosophy?

- *words* will produce *thinking*
- *thinking* will produce your *emotions/feelings*
- *feelings* will produce *decisions*
- *decisions* will produce *actions*
- *actions* will produce *habits*
- *habits* will produce *character*
- *character* will bring you to your *destiny*

THE IMPORTANCE OF IDENTITY: BECOMING A MASTER BY MASTERING YOUR MIND

Pray! Ask Father God for insight as you seek to understand our identity in Christ.

STEP OUT ON THE JOURNEY (15 MINUTES)

Review the fourth week. Encourage members to share observations, comments or ask questions.

VIDEO/TEACHING (30 MINUTES)

DRILLING DOWN (30 MINUTES)

- The ultimate key to deliverance in this life is embracing who you are in Christ–and who He is within you. Can you put into words your own identity in Christ?

- Whatever has ensnared you is not greater than God's power—and desire—to set you free! Do you believe this?

- According to 2 Cor 5:17, anyone who belongs to Christ is a new creation; the old has gone and the new has come! Have you accepted that truth? It is possible to have participants who have not yet accepted Christ as their Savior, or some may feel the need to recommit their lives to God. Offer a time of prayer, with eyes closed, and encourage those who would like to take this step to repeat after you: *Dear God in heaven, I come to you in the name of Jesus. I acknowledge to You that I am a sinner, and I am sorry for my sins and the life that I have lived; I need your forgiveness. I believe that your only begotten Son Jesus Christ shed His precious blood on the cross at Calvary and died for my sins, and I am now willing to turn from my sin. You said that if we confess the Lord our God and believe in our hearts that God raised Jesus from the dead, we will be saved. Right now I confess Jesus as the Lord of my soul. With my heart, I believe that God raised Jesus from the dead. This very moment I accept Jesus Christ as my own personal Savior and according to His Word, right now I am saved. Thank you for your free gift of salvation. In Jesus' name, amen.* Make special note of anyone who made this decision for the first time and offer them extra encouragement as well as any resources you or your church can provide.

- You learn more about who you were created to be by learning about who He is. The more time you spend learning about the nature of God, learning the ways of Christ, and keeping company with His Spirit, the more you are transformed into His likeness. How have you experienced this truth?

- How can you more fully embrace your identity in Christ? What does that look like? How do you walk that out in everyday life?

- How does this knowledge of your true identity enable you to live more authentically?

Journey Plans for the Next Week

Point out Day 21–Day 26 in the book and guide. Encourage everyone to participate fully in this journey in order to get the most out of it.

Close in Prayer

VIDEO LISTENING GUIDE

What is your definition of identity?

What breadcrumbs, or clues, can you use to discover who you are?

The greatest conversation we can have with God starts with, "Who am I? Who am I called to be?"

Personality is who you are, and it's from God.
Temperament is changeable.

You can only adjust what you address.

Identity is boundary of self—it's where I start and stop and where you start and stop.

Identity gives me a clue to my purpose.

When people call your name, what image comes to their mind?

The thing that you are pushing at is the thing that's eating you.

Who am I? Why am I here?

Where am I going? How am I going to get there?

What resources has God left for me to get it?

Who should be going with me?

What kind of legacy am I going to leave?

 *Why be a poor copy of someone else,
when you can be a very good original?*

I AM...

- God's child (see John 1:12)

- Christ's friend (see John 15:5)

- A member of Christ's Body (see 1 Cor. 12:27)

- A saint, a holy one (see Eph. 1:1)

- Redeemed and forgiven of all my sins (see Col. 1:14)

- Complete in Christ (see Col. 2:10)

- Free from condemnation (see Rom. 8:1-2)

- Assured that all things work together for good (see Rom. 8:28)

- Secure and cannot be separated from the love of God (see Rom. 8:35-39)

- A citizen of Heaven (see Phil. 3:20)

- Given a spirit of power, love and discipline (see 2 Tim. 1:7)

- Chosen and appointed by God to bear fruit (see John 15:16)

- A temple of God (see 1 Cor. 3:16)

- Seated with Christ In the heavenly realm (see Eph. 2:10)

- God's workmanship, created for good works (see Eph. 2:10)

- The apple of His eye (see Deut. 32:9-10)

Week Six

THE POWER OF WORDS:
HEALING THE HOLE IN YOUR SOUL

Pray! Ask The Word Incarnate to enlighten you regarding the power of words.

STEP OUT ON THE JOURNEY (15 MINUTES)

Review the fifth week. Encourage members to share observations, comments or ask questions.

VIDEO/TEACHING (30 MINUTES)

DRILLING DOWN (30 MINUTES)

- God's Word carries immense creative power and always accomplishes what He intends it to! Read Isaiah 55:10-11 aloud.

- Words are powerful, and can be dangerous! Life and death are in the power of the tongue. Read Proverbs 18:21. How have you experienced this truth–either on the life side of it, or the death side?

- Where are you heading, and what will it look like when you get there? Spend time this week pondering this... let your imaginations take over! Read, write, study, paint or draw what it would look like. Then line up your words and *talk* about it!

- When we read the Bible, we need to take God's Word personally. His promises are for His people, and if you have received Him as your Lord and Savior, that means you! Make God's Word personal by inserting your name in the promises He gives. What does this mean to you? How much more 'real' does this make His promises?

- What must happen in your heart for there to be a change in your mouth? How can you 'speak for a change'?

JOURNEY PLANS FOR THE NEXT WEEK

Point out Day 26–Day 30 in the book and journal. Encourage everyone to participate fully in this journey in order to get the most out of it.

CLOSE IN PRAYER

Week Six

VIDEO LISTENING GUIDE

*Words can drop like acid and
create holes in our souls.*

Your <u>brain</u> and your <u>flesh</u> don't want to go on a
spiritual journey!

> *For the word of God is quick, and powerful,
> and sharper than any two-edged sword, pierc-
> ing even to the dividing asunder of soul and
> spirit, and of the joints and marrow, and is
> a discerner of the thoughts and intents of the
> heart* (Hebrews 4:12 KJV).

<u>Favor</u> is attached to right living, living
authentically.

<u>Grace</u> is attached to wrong living, covering the
things that are inauthentic.

<u>Integrity</u> refers to being single and whole.

*The more authentic you become,
the more freedom you give to
other people to be authentic.*

*There are things you pray aside,
and others you lay aside.*

What do you want?

*The last place of your healing is where
you're living emotionally right now.*

Words are images clothed in a language.

*The soul fast is trying to get to the root of
the problem, and heal it. Then we don't
have the fruit that affects our behavior.*

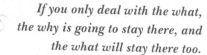
Why am I doing the things that I'm doing?

*If you only deal with the what,
the why is going to stay there, and
the what will stay there too.*

THE POWER OF DOING: GOD'S CHOSEN FAST

Pray! Ask the Holy Spirit to show you His heart about the power of doing.

STEP OUT ON THE JOURNEY (15 MINUTES)

Review the sixth week. Encourage members to share observations, comments or ask questions.

VIDEO/TEACHING (30 MINUTES)

DRILLING DOWN (30 MINUTES)

The purpose of fasting in the life of the believer is to take "self" off the throne and allow God's love to reign there instead.

- Read Isaiah 58:6-10 aloud.

- Think about and discuss God's chosen fast in light of 1 Cor. 13:1-13.

- In other words, if we don't walk in the fruit of the Spirit, then the gifts of the Spirit are useless. What is the fruit in your life from having removed the junk in your heart, the clutter from your mind, and the entanglements from your soul?

- What is different about you as a result of this 40-day Soul Fast?

- Encourage your members to pray about sharing their testimony of changes throughout this soul fast at the last meeting.

Journey Plans for the Next Week

Point out Day 31–Day 35 in the book and guide. Encourage everyone to participate fully in this journey in order to get the most out of it.

Close in Prayer

VIDEO LISTENING GUIDE

> *You cannot give God what you don't have. You've got to get in the driver's seat first, before you can be free to choose to hand control over to Him.*

We run to people who don't know who they are and ask them to tell us who we are.

You will always <u>resemble</u> those with whom you <u>assemble</u>.

The enemy doesn't <u>fight</u> what he doesn't <u>fear</u>.

What about you is the enemy fighting?

> *I don't have to be afraid of life and afraid of the enemy, because the enemy is afraid of me.*

What if you have prayed and prayed for your family, community, government, and you are the answer?

Week Eight

SEALING THE HEALING: THE CLEANSING POWER OF LOVE

Pray! Ask the Risen Lord to give you new ways to celebrate His life-changing Spirit in you.

STEP OUT ON THE JOURNEY (15 MINUTES)

Review the seventh week. Encourage members to share observations, comments or ask questions.

VIDEO/TEACHING (30 MINUTES)

DRILLING DOWN (30 MINUTES)

- Feast days and celebrations have always been significant in the life of God's people. Israel was commanded, and we as believers are still commanded, to stop and celebrate–or commemorate - and give glory to the One who brings the blessing and makes all things new. Why is this a command?

- God understood the necessity for His people to establish regular intervals to stop and reconnect, to recall their true identity in relation to their Heavenly Father and the Creator of all things. What does this reconnection do for us?

- Seal the healing of your soul by giving thanks and glorifying God for all He has done!

Journey Plans for the Next Week

Next week is the last meeting you will have with this group. Remind members that you would love to have them share their testimony at the next meeting. If you will be having a "celebration"—make sure to plan refreshments, etc.

Encourage the new leaders that you have identified to consider planning to lead a group of their own. Offer to assist them if you are able. Encourage them to pass the healing forward—until we have really healed the world by healing our own soul!

Close in Prayer

VIDEO LISTENING GUIDE

*Now abideth faith hope and love, but the greatest
of these is love* (1 Corinthians 13:13 NKJV)

> *Spiritual warfare does not disappear
> when we start to live authentically.*

Tolerance is giving people permission to be
<u>different</u>.

*Reach out beyond yourself and demonstrate
the healing power of love. We can see
the world healed through love.*

If there was one characteristic from this week that you
would choose to "champion", which one would it be
and why?

In one or two sentences, describe your
experience over the last eight weeks.

Week Nine

CELEBRATION!

Pray! Ask our Heavenly Father to show you new ways to celebrate His life-changing Spirit in you.

**This week is a time to celebrate with your members who have made great strides towards living more authentic lives. You may want to plan a celebration with festive decorations, favorite foods, music, and sharing of testimonies.

STEP OUT ON THE JOURNEY (15 MINUTES)

Review the eighth week. Encourage members to share observations, comments or ask questions.

VIDEO (15 MINUTES)

DRILLING DOWN (30 MINUTES)

- Allow time for personal testimonies; affirm the healing of each soul!
- Celebrate!

Journey Plans

This is the last meeting you will have with this group. Encourage the new leaders that you have identified to begin planning to lead a group of their own. Offer to assist them if you are able. Encourage them to pass the healing forward–until we have really healed the world by healing our own soul!

Close in Prayer

DR. TRIMM'S BLESSING

I have the courage and personal integrity to:

- Be myself
- Dream about a better life
- Wake up and live the life of my dreams
- Enjoy today and believe that tomorrow will be better than today
- Voice my opinions
- Pursue my goals
- Change my mind
- Break self-destructive activities, thoughts, and cycles of failure
- Set clear boundaries for myself and help others to respect them
- Change for the best
- Be my best
- Give my best
- Do my best

- Put my best foot forward
- Enjoy giving and receiving live
- Face and transform my fears with courage
- Seek and ask for support when I need it
- Spring free from the super-person trap
- Stop being all things to everyone
- Trust myself to know what is right for me
- Make my own decisions based on my perceptions of options
- Befriend myself
- Be kind to myself
- Be totally honest with myself
- Respect my vulnerabilities
- Heal old and current wounds
- Acquire new, good, and useful habits and eliminate the bad
- Complete unfinished business
- View my failures as life lessons
- Turn my losses into gain
- Realize that I have emotional and practical rights

- Honor my commitments
- Keep my promises
- Give myself credit for my accomplishments
- Love the little girl/boy in me
- Overcome my addictions and need for approval
- Grant myself permission to laugh out loud
- Live life out loud
- Play as hard as I can
- Dance like no one is watching
- Sing at the top of my voice
- Color outside of the lines
- Watch Mother Nature as she tucks the sun in for a good night's sleep and then turns the nightlights on for my enjoyment, security, and pleasure
- Witness the dawning of a new day as the sun rubs lingering sleepiness from its eyes
- Choose life over death
- Choose success over failure
- Live with an attitude of gratitude

- Quit being a trash receptacle and dumping bin
- Rid myself of toxic relationships
- Pursue and develop healthy and supportive relationships
- Renegotiate the terms of all relationships
- Nurture myself like I nurture others
- Take "me moments"
- Be alone without feeling lonely
- Demand that people give to me as much as I give them
- Manage my time
- Value the time that God has given me by using it wisely
- Demand others to value my time
- Be more objective about my feelings and subjective about my thoughts
- Detoxify all areas of my life
- Take an emotional enema when necessary
- Nurture others because I want to not because I have to
- Choose what is right for me

- Insist on being paid fairly for what I do
- Know when enough is enough
- Say "No" and mean it
- Put an end to toxic cycles
- Set limits and boundaries
- Say "Yes" only when I really mean it
- Have realistic expectations
- Take risks and accept change
- Live morally
- Conduct my affairs ethically
- Grow through change
- Grow through challenges
- Give others permissions to grow and be themselves
- Break glass ceilings
- Live beyond the limits
- Set new goals
- Savor the mystery of the Holy Spirit
- Pray and expect an exceptional and favorable outcome
- Meditate in order to un-clutter my mind

- Wave good-bye to guilt, self-doubt, rejection, and insecurity

- De-weed the flower bed of my thought life

- Treat myself with respect and teach others to do the same

- Fill my own cup first, and then refresh others from the overflow

- Demand excellence from others and myself

- Plan for the future but live in the present

- Value my insight, intelligence, and wisdom

- Know that I am loveable

- Celebrate the differences in others

- Make forgiveness a priority

- Accept myself just as I am now and forever

- Live within my means

- Manifest His divinity

- Breathe beyond innate fears by living in the realm of faith

- Embrace His Spirit, which is stronger and wiser than mine
- Prosper beyond my imagination
- Give more than I receive
- Give to those who can never return the favor
- Love unconditionally
- Live consciously
- Therefore, I will:
- Give God the time He needs
- Give my mind the order and peace it needs
- Give my life the discipline it needs
- Give my spirit the freedom it needs
- Give my soul the love it needs
- Give my body the nourishment and exercise it needs
- Give my voice the platform it needs
- Take a stand for what I believe
- Give myself the love and attention I need
- Pursue my dreams and accomplish my goals

- Pursue my purpose and maximize my potential
- Stand on truth and take a stand for truth
- Positively impact my generation
- Positively influence a system and/or an institution
- Live, learn, love, serve, and then leave a legacy

I am on a collision course with destiny:
I am at the Intersection of Truth; the Avenue of Opportunity; the Boulevard of Passion; and on a Street named Courage.
All lights are green. I choose to proceed.
Today, I crash and walk away with purpose, success, and nobility.
Today and always:
I alone accept and own full and total responsibility for being my genuine and true self.
Therefore,
I vow to live authentically, to grow and care for my best and nobler self that I may reflect the shimmer of God's glory and divinity.
Today, I shall be blessed with all good things.
My day shall be good.

I will have good success.

My joy, peace, prosperity, and success shall be as abundant as the stars at night.

Friendship, favor, affluence, influence, health, happiness, support, beauty, and abundant living shall be my constant companion.

I am unconditionally loved, celebrated, revered, appreciated, and honored beyond measure and human comprehension.

I make a difference in this world.

This is my contract with self.

And today, I give myself permission to push until I succeed.

Appendix A

THE 40-DAY SOUL FAST HANDBOOK

SUGGESTED GUIDELINES FOR DETOXIFYING SPIRIT, SOUL, AND BODY

BY DR. CINDY TRIMM

In consultation with
DR. PAULA WALKER M.D.

A PERSONAL WORD FROM DR. CINDY TRIMM

If you are reading this, you are taking part in the 40 Day Soul Fast. Please remember the purpose of the Soul Fast is to eliminate the toxins in your soul, not your body. However, because the body and soul are interconnected, what is good for one is good for the other! I encourage you to take this opportunity to cleanse and detox your body even as you dedicate yourself to cleansing and detoxifying your soul.

The Body of Christ is longing for detoxification on so many levels. That is demonstrated by the large number of people who have asked me for information about detoxifying their entire system as they pursue this 40 Day Soul Fast. That is why I am making this informational booklet available. I pray it will be a useful tool to help you along your "life cleansing" journey.

Remember, Jesus said, "It is not what goes into the mouth of a man that makes him unclean...but what comes out of the mouth; this makes a man unclean... whatever comes out of the mouth comes from the heart, and this is what makes a man unclean" (Matthew 11:15, 18 AMP).

If you choose to pursue a physical fast along with the soul fast, please don't become distracted or burdened by the demands of a restrictive fasting regimen. I would encourage you to prayerfully allow God to lead you into laying aside whatever is keeping you from thinking more clearly, having more energy, or pursuing Him more fully. I would suggest along with fasting unhealthy foods, you fast unhealthy thoughts—as you give up toxic eating habits, give up toxic behaviors. It is more destructive to your soul to engage in gossip or complaining than it is to eat gravy or cupcakes.

The primary aim of the 40 Day Soul Fast is to "lay aside every weight, and the sin which so easily ensnares us, and let us run with endurance the race that is set before us" (Heb. 12:1). The weights of negative thought habits and toxic verbal behaviors tie you down and keep you vulnerable to sin. The debris in your mind and the junk coming out of (not going into) your mouth are what keep you stagnated and going around in circles. These are the toxins that prevent you from running with endurance and fulfilling your divine purpose—and cause so many to abort their God-given dreams.

If exercising the discipline of fasting unhealthy foods will help you be more mindful of exercising the discipline of fasting unhealthy thoughts, then let the two work together synergistically to help you bring your spirit, soul, and body into alignment. It is for this reason I am making this guide available—to help you learn to cleanse and renew your body even as you cleanse and renew your mind! May you be *empowered for life* and *empowered to live beyond your limits!*

SCRIPTURE REFERENCES

When this vision came to me, I, Daniel, had been in mourning for three whole weeks. All that time I had eaten no rich food. No meat or wine crossed my lips, and I used no fragrant lotions until those three weeks had passed (Daniel 10:2-3 NLT).

This is the kind of fast day I'm after: to break the chains of injustice, get rid of exploitation in the workplace; free the oppressed; cancel debts. What I'm interested in seeing you do is: sharing your food with the hungry, inviting the homeless poor into your homes, putting clothes on the shivering ill-clad, being available to your own families.

Do this and the lights will turn on, and your lives will turn around at once. Your righteousness will pave your way. The God of glory will secure your passage. Then when you pray, God will answer. You'll call out for help and I'll say, "Here I am."

A Full Life in the Emptiest of Places

> *If you get rid of unfair practices, quit blaming victims, quit gossiping about other people's sins, if you are generous with the hungry and start giving yourselves to the down-and-out, your lives will begin to glow in the darkness, your shadowed lives will be bathed in sunlight. I will always show you where to go. I'll give you a full life in the emptiest of places—firm muscles, strong bones. You'll be like a well-watered garden, a gurgling spring that never runs dry. You'll use the old rubble of past lives to build anew, rebuild the foundations from out of your past. You'll be known as those who can fix anything, restore old ruins, rebuild and renovate, make the community livable again* (Isaiah 58:9-12).

It's not what goes into your body that defiles you; you are defiled by what comes from your heart (Mark 7:15 NLT).

Can't you see that the food you put into your body cannot defile you? Food doesn't go into your heart, but only passes through the stomach and then goes into the sewer." (By saying this, he declared that every kind of food is acceptable in God's eyes.)

And then he added, "It is what comes from inside that defiles you. For from within, out of a person's heart, come evil thoughts, sexual immorality, theft, murder, adultery, greed, wickedness, deceit, lustful desires, envy, slander, pride, and foolishness. All these vile things come from within; they are what defile you" (Mark 7:18-23 NLT).

We work to feed our appetites. Meanwhile our souls go hungry (Ecclesiastes 6:7 MSG).

THE "FAST" WAY TO HEALING AND HEALTH

Some people wear out one set of teeth digging their way to the grave, only to buy a false set of teeth to complete the task of eating themselves to death.

—AUTHOR UNKNOWN

Fasting—traditionally seen as a spiritual activity—is increasingly being used as a method to improve physical, mental, and emotional health. It is an ever-increasing belief that fasting not only helps to relieve the body of toxins, but also stimulates and increases spiritual awareness and produces growth hormones, which postpones the aging process. The search for health goes on unceasingly, and fasting has helped many to achieve it.

Contrary to what our minds may tell us, the body can function for seven days without water and forty days without food. I am not asking you to go forty days without food, but I do encourage you to practice one of the fasting options offered below for the duration of the 40 Day Soul Fast. I believe your soul will benefit from any cleansing taking place in your body—and vice versa! *"Beloved, I pray that you may prosper in all things and be in health, just as your soul prospers"* (3 John 1:2 NKJV).

The following information is intended to give you a variety of options you can pursue, some general guidelines to follow, an array of basic information to consider, and other helpful tools you can use to cleanse your life—body, soul, and spirit.

Cleanse and nourish your body by avoiding all toxic products and unwholesome foods and hydrating sufficiently—no less than eight glasses of water per day!

Cleanse and nourish your soul by avoiding all toxic media and unwholesome entertainment—hydrate your soul by drinking from the fountain of the Word daily!

Cleanse and nourish your spirit by avoiding toxic places and unwholesome people—hydrate your spirit by praising and worshiping God whenever possible.

Be good to yourself—your true, authentic self—your soul.

Read The Creed provided at the back of this booklet everyday for the next 40 days.

*For the next 40 days, set aside 40 minutes each day to invest in the life of your soul.

Weekly:

1. Listen to each week's video lesson.

Daily:

2. Set aside a designated time and place to read the daily entry in the book and

respond to the action steps in the companion journal as well as the phone app.

3. Pray that the Lord will reveal to you the specific toxins cluttering your own soul.

4. Praise God for the answers, solutions, and guidance He has promised.

5. Recite The Creed at the start of each day.

Detox Your Whole Self

Any good health program should include a system for detoxifying—or cleansing—the body of toxins. Detoxing is the process of removing harmful toxins from the body—the whole body—including the heart and mind.

You haven't completely detoxed until you've detoxed in the following ways:

Psychologically

An individual's psychological state of being will be a determining factor in overall physical health. People who are constantly under stress from career, lifestyle, financial, or marital pressures need to take time out to give not only the body a rest, but also the mind. Create space for "down-time" to relieve the mind of anything that causes undue stress and meditate on positive things.

It has been found that psychological and emotional symptoms are directly associated with excess toxins in the body. Create a peaceful atmosphere for yourself while focusing on detoxifying your system. Here are some pointers:

- Be aware of internal dialogue
- Refuse negativity
- Think positive thoughts
- Change the things you can
- Accept the things you cannot change

Emotionally

The heavy demands that we are all subject to in today's world may give rise to stress, anxiety, mood swings, depression, tension, poor memory, forgetfulness, irritability, negativity, mental exhaustion, etc. and may render us less objective and effective in handling the affairs of the day. As you detox your body, detox your thoughts:

- Create a peaceful environment—incorporate fresh flowers.

- Clear your home and work environment of unnecessary clutter.

- Give away whatever you haven't used or worn in the past year.

- Play uplifting music in lieu of turning on the television.

- Just play! Play with your pet, play games, play an instrument.

- Be creative. Be adventurous. Explore a new craft or hobby.

- Watch a life-affirming movie.

- Exercise every day (ride a bike, take a brisk walk outdoors).

- Focus on fresh air! Get outside whenever you can!

- Take steam baths/saunas twice weekly.

- Take a bath in Epsom salts or baking soda to draw out impurities.

- Drink a minimum of eight glasses of water each day.

- Take time to rest and reflect daily.

- Smile at others and laugh at yourself.

- Hug your loved ones.
- Give thanks.

A NOTE FROM DR. PAULA WALKER

After prayer and consideration of the various factors involved in regards to the unique circumstances of the many individuals participating in the cleansing program (such as their health status, medication regimens, high-demand work schedules, rigorous lifestyles, personal fasting history, and so on), here are my suggestions for undergoing a long-term cleansing-type fast.

I do not recommend total fasting from food and liquid, especially water. The body needs at least two quarts of water each day to sustain life. The body can only go a few days without water. That being said, total fasting would be unsafe.

For the purpose of a 40-day fast, I do not recommend limiting intake to water-only. While water only fasting has therapeutic benefits in certain cases where there is inflammation in the body (such as in cases of Osteoarthritis, Lupus, Rheumatoid Arthritis, Fibromyalgia, etc.), in general, water-only fasts are not well tolerated for extended periods of time and the liver (the detoxifying organ of the body) is mostly unsupported during a water-only fast. Also, water-only fasts are often associated with an unpleasant weakness that is counterproductive for active individuals. Furthermore, water-only fasts may lead to low potassium levels. Low potassium can cause life threatening cardiac arrhythmias or abnormal heart rhythms. For these reasons, I would suggest eliminating this type of fast as an option.

Some options I would suggest for a 40 day fasting period would be the following:

For the Experienced Faster: The Master Cleanser Fast

Only consume water and the Master Cleanser beverage (recipe provided below) throughout the entire 40-day process. If an individual is on medication, he or she *must* consult his or her physician and follow the medication recommendations put forth by his or her doctor. Physician consultation is necessary because some medications will preempt one's ability to fast while other medications can be safely taken during a fast.

For the Intermediate Faster: A Partial Fast

This option can include a sun up to sun down alternative—the faster can eat from 6:00 A.M. to 6:00 P.M. and then do a water-only fast from 6:00 P.M. to 6:00 A.M. With this model, eating is done during the day when the faster is actively engaged in activities and can use the additional dietary fuel and burn the excess calories, but this option can also be implemented vice versa with fasting occurring from 6:00 A.M. to 6:00 P.M. with eating beginning after 6:00 P.M.

Or, otherwise on this partial fast, the individual may eat only fruits and vegetables (during a specified time window) and drink water only during the entire 40 day fast; organic fruits and vegetables should be used when possible. The fruits and vegetables that are consumed should be consumed from 8:00 A.M. to 12:00 noon only. The individual can eat any variety or version of fruits and vegetables. After 12:00 noon, the individual should abstain from all whole fruit and vegetable intake. During the remaining 20 hours of the day (12:00 P.M. to 8:00 A.M.), preferably only water should be consumed. The Master Cleanser beverage may also be consumed, if the faster desires a cleansing, healthful beverage as an alternative to water. During the 20 hour water-only fasting period of each day, if the faster experiences overwhelming cravings that are unsatisfied by water or the Master Cleanser beverage, he or she should go ahead and have a serving of fruit and/or vegetables at that time and as needed.

Again, if an individual is on medication, he or she should consult his or her physician and follow the medication recommendations put forth by his or her doctor. Physician consultation is necessary because some medications will preempt one's ability to fast while other medications can be safely taken during a fast.

During this partial fast, it is suggested that no other food items be consumed besides any variety or version of fresh fruits and vegetables. No other beverages, other than those stated, should be consumed. All sodas, fruit juices, sweet tea, lemonade, coffee, lattes, and other drinks are to be avoided.

For the Beginner Faster: The Daniel Fast

The individual would eat no meat, no sweets and no bread. Throughout the 40 days, the individual would eat any variety or version of fruits, vegetables, legumes (peas, beans, nuts, etc) and certain dietary fibers, such as brown rice, steel-cut oatmeal (without butter, sugar, or other condiments), and drink water only as desired throughout the day. Meal variation may include a vegetable/legume plate with several servings of vegetables constituting one meal (e.g. squash, green beans, cabbage, and black eye peas, etc.), salads, vegetable soups, whole fruits, grilled vegetables, bean soup, vegetable and bean casserole, etc.

If an individual is on medication, he or she should continue to take them, unless directed otherwise by a physician. Physician consultation is necessary because some medications will preempt one's ability to fast while other medications can be safely taken during a fast.

This fast is recommended for the beginning faster as well as for Type II Diabetics, who have received medical clearance from their doctors to participate in the fast. Type II Diabetics should consult their physician about possible adjustments to their blood-sugar lowering medication regimen during the fasting season to avoid episodes of hypoglycemia or low blood sugar.

For Fasters of All Levels: The Juice Fast

For this type of fast, the individual will need a juicer and a variety of fresh fruits and vegetables. Juice fasting is beneficial for the body. It supports the liver and the detoxification process. It's less strenuous and it doesn't produce any undesirable weakness or fatigue. No solid foods will be consumed on this fast, just the juice of fresh fruits and vegetables and water. Organic produce is preferable and should be used whenever possible. Again, juices should be prepared freshly. No commercial fruit or vegetable juices should be used during the fast such as V-8, Tropicana, Snapple, etc.

If an individual is on medications, he or she should consult his or her physician and follow the medication recommendations put forth by his or her doctor. Physician consultation is necessary because some medications will preempt one's ability to fast while other medications can be safely taken during a fast.

For fresh fruit and vegetable juice recipes, I recommend Dr. Don Colbert's book entitled *Toxic Relief*. The book may be purchased at any book retailer.

All of the above fasts are easy on the digestive system and will give the gastrointestinal system a Sabbath from the work and energy of digesting food. Since energy will not be expended by digesting dense foods, more energy will be available for other activities. In essence, the faster will feel energized! More importantly, all of the above fasts represent a sacrifice of some kind so the fasting option choice is a personal one, based on health status and the divine guidance of the Holy Spirit. God will honor the sacrifice!

Lastly, as part of the guidelines, please be advised that if you have questions or concerns about anything related to your health, you must consult your physician prior to beginning any type of fast. Any individual who has health issues or concerns in general about his or her physical ability to fast should consult his or her physician before beginning the fast.

The above fasting options are offered solely as suggestions. Anyone who follows them does so voluntarily and is advised to consult their physician beforehand. Since each individual will react differently to each fasting option, each person must use his or her own judgment as to its use and continuation throughout the proposed 40-day period.

FASTING GUIDELINES

Prior to beginning any type of fast, each participant should consult with his or her doctor.

As wonderful of a tool as fasting is for health and cleansing and detoxification purposes, there are some individuals who have certain conditions where fasting is contraindicated or prohibited.

Please keep the following in mind if you are considering the pursuit of a fast:

- Do not fast if you are pregnant or nursing.

- Do not fast if you have a serious illness like cancer, AIDS, Anorexia Nervosa, Leukemia, severe anemia, or if you are emaciated or malnourished as the result of another illness.

- Do not fast if you are a Type I Diabetic or Insulin-Dependent Diabetic.

- All Type II Diabetics (and some Type II Diabetics on insulin) should especially inquire of his or her physician about the feasibility of fasting and about any possible adjustments to the insulin/blood sugar-lowering medication regimen during the fasting period since the blood sugars tend to be lower during a fast. If diabetics receive medical clearance to do the fast, they should continue home monitoring of blood sugars throughout the fast as directed by their physician. Note: Of the options listed, the Daniel Fast is the most suitable option for Type II Diabetics, who have received medical clearance.

- Do not fast if you are taking a diuretic (or "water pill"). Diuretics precipitate loss of water and electrolytes like potassium. Do not fast if you have liver or kidney disease; the liver is the detoxifying organ of the body and the kidneys aid in the elimination of waste via the urine. If either of these organs is impaired, it will be difficult to obtain the usual benefits from fasting, and you may exacerbate your medical condition.

- Do not fast if you have congestive heart failure or a diagnosed cardiac arrhythmia.

- Do not fast if you are on certain medications like prednisone, narcotics, antidepressants, or diuretics. You should refrain from fasting if you are taking any of these medications. However, there are other medications that can be safely taken during a fast. Please consult your health care provider when considering a fast to determine if fasting is right for you.

Medications should not be discontinued abruptly. If a fasting participant is on medicine, he or she should consult his or her physician regarding possible adjustments to the medication regimen during the fasting regimen.

If the participant develops exacerbation of an existing medical illness or begins to develop adverse reactions or worrisome symptoms of any kind, he or she should discontinue the fast immediately and consult his or her physician immediately.

Distilled water is used for the Master Cleanser recipe; otherwise, if the faster is consuming water for hydration purposes with the other fasting options, spring or filtered water may be consumed.

Organic produce should be used whenever possible where fruits and vegetables are listed in the fasting options.

Fasters should be compassionate and gentle with themselves. During the fast, if they fall off the wagon and consume a restricted food or dietary item, they should acknowledge the detour (and enjoy it) and get back on the fast as soon as possible.

How you end a fast is just as important as how you start and conduct one. A typical post-fasting regimen, for breaking a fast, would look like the following. Starting with the first day after the fast:

> Day 1: Eat fresh fruit, especially fruits with
> the highest water content because these

are the easiest to digest and assimilate. Note: On Day 1, avoid tropical fruits, such as pineapples and papayas, since these contain strong enzymes that might upset your stomach.

Day 2: You may have a combination of fresh fruits and vegetables throughout the day. For instance, you might choose to have fresh fruit for breakfast followed by vegetable soup for lunch and dinner.

Day 3: You will follow a similar diet as outlined for Day 2.

Day 4: You may add to the various fruits and vegetable soups a salad and/or a baked potato.

Day 5: Building on the diet from the previous four days, you may now introduce a small serving of lean (preferably organic) meat, such as chicken, turkey, or fish.

MASTER CLEANSER RECIPE*

The most convenient way to make the Master Cleanser beverage is by the gallon—that way it will last throughout the day.

You will need:

> The juice of 10 fresh organic lemons
> 1/8 tsp to 1/4 Tsp of cayenne pepper
> 1 1/3 cup of grade B maple syrup
> 1 gallon of distilled, purified, or spring water [distilled water tends to yield a deeper cleanse and is often preferred for this reason]

Take the gallon of water and remove two cups of the water and place it aside in a separate, clean pitcher. To the remaining water in the gallon of distilled/spring water add the lemon juice, grade B maple syrup, and cayenne pepper. Afterwards, reintroduce the two cups of water to the gallon of distilled/spring water until the gallon bottle is full; lastly shake the gallon bottle to thoroughly mix the contents. The Master Cleanser beverage is now ready to be consumed. Additional grade B maple syrup may be added to taste. Refrigerate the unused portion of the Master Cleanser beverage to maintain its freshness.

One may drink as much of the Master Cleanser beverage as desired.

Here is the recipe for one 16 oz. glass or mug (may be consumed cold or hot):

> 2 Tbsp fresh lemon juice (approx. 1/2 lemon)
> 2 Tbsp genuine grade B maple syrup
> 1/10 Tsp cayenne pepper (red pepper)
> 10-16 oz distilled, spring, or purified water

Combine the lemon juice, maple syrup, and cayenne pepper in a large glass or mug and fill with cold or hot water.

How to Break the Master Cleanser Fast

Day 1 and Day 2: Drink several 8 oz. glasses of fresh orange juice as desired throughout the day. The orange juice prepares the digestive system to properly digest and assimilate regular food. Drink it slowly. If there has been any digestive difficulty prior to or during the change over, extra water may be taken with the orange juice.

Day 3: Orange juice in the morning. Raw fruit should be consumed for lunch. Fruit or vegetable salad at night. You are now ready to eat normally.

(See Burroughs, Stanley. *The Master Cleanser,* Reno, NV: Burroughs Books, 1976.)

POWERFUL JUICE COMBINATIONS
By Paul C. Bragg

1. Beet, celery, and alfalfa sprouts
2. Cabbage, celery, and apple
3. Cabbage, cucumber, celery, tomato, spinach, and basil
4. Tomato, carrot, and mint
5. Carrot, celery, watercress, garlic, and wheatgrass
6. Grapefruit, orange, and lemon
7. Beet, parsley, celery, carrot, mustard greens, and garlic
8. Beet, celery, dulse, and carrot
9. Cucumber, carrot, and mint
10. Carrot, celery, parsley, onion, cabbage, and sweet basil
11. Carrot and coconut milk

12. Carrot, broccoli, lemon, and cayenne

13. Carrot, cauliflower, and rosemary

14. Apple, carrot, radish, and ginger

15. Apple, pineapple, and mint

16. Apple, papaya, and grapes

17. Papaya, cranberries, and apple

18. Grape, cherry, and apple

19. Watermelon (include seeds)

20. Leafy greens, broccoli, and apple

21. Beets, celery, and carrots

22. Asparagus, carrot, and mint

23. Watercress, cucumber, and garlic

24. Mission figs and water

25. Your own favorite combinations

Note: During your juice fast, in addition to the above drinks, you may add the following beverages:

- Hot water, honey, lemon and cayenne pepper
- Herbal teas
- Aloe vera (look for the fasting or detox formula)

- Noni Juice

CONSECRATION SHOPPING LIST

Please read all labels before purchasing. Do not purchase foods containing refined sugars, artificial sweeteners, excessive salt and/or additives. Please consult your doctor (especially those on medication) before you alter your diet or initiate a fast.

Vegetables

Avocados, Leeks, Carrots, Yams, Bean Sprouts, Cabbage, Broccoli, Radishes, Beets, Peppers, Cucumber, Watercress, Potatoes, Squashes, Plantain, Egg Plant, Celery, Kohlrabi, Cauliflower, Zucchini, Peas, Turnips, Pumpkin, Brussels Sprouts, Onions, Sweet Potatoes, Parsnips, Artichokes, Asparagus, Tomatoes

Salad/Green Leafy Vegetables

Romaine Lettuce, Chives, Lamb's Lettuce, Curly Endive, Oak Leaf, Butter Head Lettuce, Boston Lettuce, Radicchio, Watercress, Coriander, Spinach, Swiss Chard, Kale, Spinach Beet, Mixed Swiss Chard, Collard Greens, Chicory

Fruit

Apples, Tangerines, Apricots, Grapes, Blackberries, Cherries, Lemons, Cranberries, Strawberries,

Grapefruit, Pears, Plums, Greengages, Guavas, Pineapples, Melons (eat alone), Kiwi Fruit, Peaches, Mangoes, Star Fruit, Limes, Papaya, Currents, Cranberries, Gooseberries

Breads/Cereals/Grains

Spelt, Barley, Sprouted Grains, Ezekiel Bread, Pumpernickel, Rye, Oat, Millet, Quinoa, Amaranth, Buckwheat, Wheat Germ, Brown Rice, Wild Rice, Basmati Rice

Nuts/Seeds

Almond, Cashew, Pistachio, Walnut, Brazil, Filbert (Hazel Nut), Macadamia, Pecan, Pine Nut, Sunflower Seeds, Pumpkin Seeds, Sesame Seeds

Herbs/Spices

Fresh Ginger, Garlic, Cilantro, Dill, Chives, Bay Leaves, Basil, Coriander, Oregano, Thyme, Parsley, Marjoram, Tarragon, Mint, Rosemary, Sage

Legumes/Beans/Sprouts

Adzuki Beans, Kidney Beans, Green Beans, Navy Beans, Pole Beans, String Beans, Lentils, Chick-Peas, Red Beans, Mung Beans, Broad Beans, Yam Beans, Wax Beans, Black-Eyed Beans, Butter Beans, Cannelloni Beans, Lima Beans, Pinto Beans, Haricot Beans,

Soy Beans (Edamame), Alfalfa Sprouts, Bean Sprouts, Broccoli Sprouts

Dried Fruits

Dates, Figs, Prunes, Raisins

Dairy Options

Almond Milk, Rice Milk, Goat Cheese, Natural Yogurt

Drink List

Purified Water, Herbal or Green Teas (including Yerba Mate and Rooibos), Fresh Vegetable Juices, Fresh Fruit Juices, Green Drinks, Noni Juice, Hot Water and Lemon

Sweetners

Honey, Agave, Molasses, Stevia (natural sweetener from the Stevia flower)

Other

Free Roaming Hen Eggs, Sea Vegetables, Nori, Wakame, TVP (Texturized Vegetable Protein), Seitan, Tofu, Hummus, Veggie Cheese, Olive Oil, Agar, Safflower Oil, Sesame Oil, Apple Cider Vinegar, Natural Mayonnaise, Fish, Ryvita Crackers, Ghee, Miso, Tempeh, Natto, Tahini, Roasted Barley

(Coffee alternative), Sesame Butter, Smart Balance, Shoyo, Postum (Coffee alternative), Chicory (Coffee alternative)

Seasoning/Condiments

Miso, Tamari, Soy Sauce, Vege-Sal, Braggs Liquid Aminos, Allspice, Cayenne Pepper, Cinnamon, Ginger, Cloves, Tofu Spreads, Mustard, Saffron, Sea Salt, Turmeric, Paprika, Balsamic Vinegar/Oil (makes a delicious salad dressing), Other Natural Herbs and Spices

Supplements

ChlorOxygen Enzymes (consume with every meal), Cell Food Probiotic (upon rising), Omega 3 Spirulina, CoQ10 Olive Leaf, Garlic Tabs Cayenne, Chromium Picolinate Colloidal Minerals and Selenium, A Good Multivitamin Grape Seed Extract

Liver Tonic

Black Grapes
Fresh Garlic/Garlic Tablets
Pure Carrot/Beet/Celery Juice (3 times per week)

Kidney Tonic

Cranberry Tablet Supplement
Hot Water/Molasses/Braggs Apple Cider Vinegar

Hot Water/Lemon/Braggs Apple Cider Vinegar/
Cayenne/Grade B Maple Syrup

Foods To Avoid

- Salt
- Refined Sugar
- Refined or Prepackaged Foods (frozen dinners or prepared dinners from a box)
- Wheat/Wheat Products (including refined breads)
- Most Snack Foods
- Dairy Products/Cow's Milk (full of steroids/growth hormones)
- Fried Foods
- Fast Foods
- Red Meats
- Processed Luncheon Meats
- Chicken
- Pork
- Shell Fish
- Mushrooms (full of fungus)
- Oranges (too acidic)

- Peanuts
- Chocolates
- Baked Goods (cakes/cookies/pies)
- Candy
- Sodas
- Ocean Spray Juices (they are not all 100%)
- Carbonated Water
- Coffee

SAMPLE DAILY MEAL PLAN

Eat six times daily instead of three.
Take enzymes with each meal.
Drink herbal or green tea throughout the day.

Upon Rising

Drink Hot Water and Lemon
Take your Probiotic, Cell Food, and ChlorOxyen
A half hour later drink Noni Juice or other Green Drink

Breakfast Options (6:00 A.M.–9:00 A.M.)

Oatmeal or Rice Cereal and Fresh Fruit
with Almond Milk
Poached or Hardboiled Eggs with Toast
(see list of suggested breads)
Fresh Fruit with Natural Yogurt garnished
with Raw Almonds or Walnuts

Mid Morning Snack Options

Fresh Fruit
Rice Cake with Almond Butter
Dried Fruit & Nuts (no peanuts)

Lunch Options (12:00 P.M.–2:00 P.M.)

Green Salad, Fish, Steamed Vegetables
Brown Rice and Beans or Lentils, Fresh
Vegetables
Fresh Vegetable Salad, Baked Sweet Potato
or Yam
Sardine Salad on Toast, Raw Vegetables
Broth-Based Soup (not creamy), Fresh
Salad

Mid Afternoon Snack Options

Fresh Fruit

Vegetable Salad
Edamame
Nuts and Dried Fruit
Rice Cake

Dinner (5:00 P.M.–7:00 P.M.)

Brown Rice with Steamed Vegetables and
Green Salad
Tofu or Fish, Baked Yam, Fresh Vegetables

Night Snack

Melon
Warm Rice or Almond Milk

REFRESHING/INVIGORATING BEVERAGES

Lemon, Maple Syrup, and Pinch of Cayenne (see Master Cleanser recipe)
Herbal or Green Teas

Be sure to consume the following on a daily basis:

- Hot water and lemon upon rising (alter-
  nate with Noni)
- Raw vegetables x3
- Water x8
- Fresh fruit x3

- Fresh green salad x3
- Whole grain x2
- Beans/seeds/nuts/grains x2
- Protein x3
- Kelp supplement x1
- Multivitamin (read label)
- Garlic tabs (read label)
- Probiotics x2
- Cell food x3
- Chloroxygen x2
- Olive leaf x3
- Coloidal minerals x2
- Cayenne x3
- Chromimum picolinate x2
- Flaxseed x3
- Noni x2

Upon rising/before retiring—alternate with hot water and lemon.

WHAT TO EXPECT

You may experience some of the following symptoms as the body rids itself of toxins:

- Fuzzy/coated tongue
- Headache
- Irritability
- Increase bowel movement
- Constipation
- Change in skin tone
- Nausea
- Break-outs
- Change in body scent
- Bad breath

DO'S FOR BODY MAINTENANCE

- Take cold showers/baths daily
- Dry skin brushing with loofah brush (exfoliates skin and increases circulation)
- Self massage
- Maintain peaceful environment
- Exercise (brisk walking outdoors)

- Steam baths/sauna (twice weekly)
- Bathe twice weekly in Epsom salts or baking soda (draws out impurities)

Do's for Spiritual Maintenance

- Daily Scripture reading
- Prayer
- Journaling
- Personal devotions/meditations

Most importantly, throughout the fasting process, be reminded of the following benefits:

- Spiritual rejuvenation
- Vital energies are liberated from the laborious task of digestion and redirected to healing and repairing the body's tissues.
- Mental alertness and centeredness
- Physical healing, emotional wellbeing
- Can be used as a preventive/curative measure for a chronic condition
- Alleviates chronic fatigue
- Increases energy, endurance, and longevity

- Regulates bowel movements and sleep patterns

MAKE A DECISION TO LEAD A HEALTHY LIFESTYLE

A decision to lead a healthy lifestyle requires a change of mindset and a commitment on your part.

Look at the statement of commitment below and check off the steps that you will take on the road to wellness and healthful living.

I will change my diet and lifestyle in the following ways:

- Eliminate red meat

- Eliminate dairy and fried foods

- Reduce salt, sugar, and alcohol

- Eliminate nicotine and caffeine

- Increase intake of beans and grains

- Increase intake of fruits and salads

- Increase intake of steamed, stir-fried, baked, and grilled vegetables

- Eliminate re-fried foods

- Substitute high fat, sugary, and salty snacks with healthy alternatives

- Detox at least twice a year
- Fast at least once a month
- Rid my life and environment of all waste and clutter
- Spend 30 minutes every day walking outdoors
- Invest quality time each day in something that brings me joy
- Show the people I love how much they mean to me daily
- Let the Lord know how much I appreciate all He's doing in my life

TAKE THE CREED

Read this creed aloud for the next 40 days. You will gain confidence and courage, and you will see marvelous things beginning to happen to you, in you, and around you. Dare to live the life of your dreams!

I have the courage and personal integrity to:

- Be myself
- Dream about a better life
- Wake up and live the life of my dreams

- Enjoy today and believe that tomorrow will be better than today
- Voice my opinions
- Pursue my goals
- Change my mind
- Break self-destructive activities, thoughts, and cycles of failure
- Set clear boundaries for myself and help others to respect them
- Change for the best
- Be my best
- Give my best
- Do my best
- Put my best foot forward
- Enjoy giving and receiving live
- Face and transform my fears with courage
- Seek and ask for support when I need it
- Spring free from the super-person trap
- Stop being all things to everyone
- Trust myself to know what is right for me

- Make my own decisions based on my perceptions of options
- Befriend myself
- Be kind to myself
- Be totally honest with myself
- Respect my vulnerabilities
- Heal old and current wounds
- Acquire new, good, and useful habits and eliminate the bad
- Complete unfinished business
- View my failures as life lessons
- Turn my losses into gain
- Realize that I have emotional and practical rights
- Honor my commitments
- Keep my promises
- Give myself credit for my accomplishments
- Love the little girl/boy in me
- Overcome my addictions and need for approval
- Grant myself permission to laugh out loud

- Live life out loud
- Play as hard as I can
- Dance like no one is watching
- Sing at the top of my voice
- Color outside of the lines
- Watch Mother Nature as she tucks the sun in for a good night's sleep and then turns the nightlights on for my enjoyment, security, and pleasure
- Witness the dawning of a new day as the sun rubs lingering sleepiness from its eyes
- Choose life over death
- Choose success over failure
- Live with an attitude of gratitude
- Quit being a trash receptacle and dumping bin
- Rid myself of toxic relationships
- Pursue and develop healthy and supportive relationships
- Renegotiate the terms of all relationships
- Nurture myself like I nurture others

- Take "me moments"
- Be alone without feeling lonely
- Demand that people give to me as much as I give them
- Manage my time
- Value the time that God has given me by using it wisely
- Demand others to value my time
- Be more objective about my feelings and subjective about my thoughts
- Detoxify all areas of my life
- Take an emotional enema when necessary
- Nurture others because I want to not because I have to
- Choose what is right for me
- Insist on being paid fairly for what I do
- Know when enough is enough
- Say "No" and mean it
- Put an end to toxic cycles
- Set limits and boundaries
- Say "Yes" only when I really mean it

- Have realistic expectations
- Take risks and accept change
- Live morally
- Conduct my affairs ethically
- Grow through change
- Grow through challenges
- Give others permissions to grow and be themselves
- Break glass ceilings
- Live beyond the limits
- Set new goals
- Savor the mystery of the Holy Spirit
- Pray and expect an exceptional and favorable outcome
- Meditate in order to un-clutter my mind
- Wave good-bye to guilt, self-doubt, rejection, and insecurity
- De-weed the flower bed of my thought life
- Treat myself with respect and teach others to do the same

- Fill my own cup first, and then refresh others from the overflow

- Demand excellence from others and myself

- Plan for the future but live in the present

- Value my insight, intelligence, and wisdom

- Know that I am loveable

- Celebrate the differences in others

- Make forgiveness a priority

- Accept myself just as I am now and forever

- Live within my means

- Manifest His divinity

- Breathe beyond innate fears by living in the realm of faith

- Embrace His Spirit, which is stronger and wiser than mine

- Prosper beyond my imagination

- Give more than I receive

- Give to those who can never return the favor

- Love unconditionally
- Live consciously
- Therefore, I will:
- Give God the time He needs
- Give my mind the order and peace it needs
- Give my life the discipline it needs
- Give my spirit the freedom it needs
- Give my soul the love it needs
- Give my body the nourishment and exercise it needs
- Give my voice the platform it needs
- Take a stand for what I believe
- Give myself the love and attention I need
- Pursue my dreams and accomplish my goals
- Pursue my purpose and maximize my potential
- Stand on truth and take a stand for truth
- Positively impact my generation
- Positively influence a system and/or an institution

- Live, learn, love, serve, and then leave a legacy

I am on a collision course with destiny:

- I am at the Intersection of Truth; the Avenue of Opportunity; the Boulevard of Passion; and on a Street named Courage.

- All lights are green. I choose to proceed.

- Today, I crash and walk away with purpose, success, and nobility.

Today and always:

- I alone accept and own full and total responsibility for being my genuine and true self.

Therefore,

- I vow to live authentically, to grow and care for my best and nobler self that I may reflect the shimmer of God's glory and divinity.

- Today, I shall be blessed with all good things.

- My day shall be good.

- I will have good success.

- My joy, peace, prosperity, and success shall be as abundant as the stars at night.

- Friendship, favor, affluence, influence, health, happiness, support, beauty, and abundant living shall be my constant companion.

- I am unconditionally loved, celebrated, revered, appreciated, and honored beyond measure and human comprehension.

- I make a difference in this world.

- This is my contract with self.

- And today, I give myself permission to push until I succeed.

_____

Signed

_____

Dated

For More Information

For information about other resources and the work of Dr. Cindy Trimm please visit www.cindy-trimm.com

Connect with Dr. Trimm: Twitter/@cindytrimm

Dr. Cindy Trimm has dedicated her life to serving God and humanity. A former senator and best-selling author, Dr. Trimm is a sought-after empowerment specialist, revolutionary thinker, and transformational leader. She has garnered a distinguished reputation as a catalyst for change and voice of hope to the nations. Dr. Trimm travels worldwide, partnering with social, spiritual and civic leaders, equipping millions to discover purpose, maximize potential, and leave a positive footprint through their lives. Viewing this world as a global village, she continues to initiate strategic interdisciplinary forums, as well as host conferences and summits designed to develop practical solutions toward healing humanity of its deeply rooted social and spiritual ills. Her best-selling books include: *The 40 Day Soul Fast, Reclaim Your Soul, The Prosperous Soul, The Prayer Warrior's Way, The Art of War for Spiritual Battle, Commanding Your Morning,* and *Rules of Engagement.*

Dr. Cindy Trimm
www.cindytrimm.com
Empowering You for Life!

Appendix B

24 QUESTIONS:

1. Who am I outside of the roles I play?

2. What are my long-term goals?

3. What should I be doing with my life right now?

4. What are my strengths?

5. What are my weaknesses?

6. What direction will my life go if I continue doing what I'm doing?

7. How can I be sure I am in the right place, doing the right thing?

8. What is my purpose?

9. Who should I be partnering with?

10. What resources are available for me to accomplish my goals?

11. Do I like the person I've become?

12. What do I really want to achieve in this lifetime?

13. What brings me my greatest joy?

14. What am I really passionate about?

15. What frustrates me most or makes me sad?

16. If I could do something other than what I am doing now, what would that be?

17. If I could live somewhere else, where would that be?

18. Do these things that I do and am involved with make me feel good and happy?

19. Are my relationships mutually beneficial and symbiotic?

20. Is there room for improvement in my relationships?

21. What have I accomplished so far with my life? Is it enough?

22. If I could do one thing different, what would it be?

23. After my death, will future generations know that I lived?

24. How do I want people to remember me?

Empowering You for Life!

Looking for *More?*

Please visit me online at www.soulfastmovement.com for more tools and resources to nurture the life of your soul. If you want to take part in the Soul Fast Movement, please go to www.soulfastmovement.com to find out how you can get involved, enroll in our ongoing programs, or participate in a guided, interactive 40 Day Soul Fast. Two times per year, I host an eight-week program when I personally coach you through each of the 40 Characteristics via my weekly empowerment broadcast, daily video blog, and downloadable phone app. There you also will find a *40 Day Soul Fast Cleansing Guide,* a free "Dynamic Life Questionnaire," an online community where you can always continue the conversation, as well as other soul-enhancing resources.

Let's do life together! Join with me as I endeavor to heal the world by healing the souls of individuals—empowering them to impact their communities and nations all across the globe. Every soul is significant and influences the world in countless ways. Never doubt that what you do *does* make a difference! You could be the answer someone else is looking for. Don't wait another day to step up to the plate—the world's next homerun could be depending on you to make the pitch. Pitch life. Pitch healing!

I value you and what you bring to the game. Let's make a difference and bring healing wherever we are. Let's make this life a winning proposition for all. For more about soul healing and empowerment, please visit me online. Join the soul healing movement or create your own. If you are interested in pioneering the unexplored frontiers of your own destiny, enroll in my signature *Executive Life Coaching* personal and professional achievement program, or register to attend a Trimm University intensive school of leadership, prayer, or ministry.

As always, I look forward to empowering you for life!

DR. CINDY TRIMM

About Dr. Cindy Trimm

A best-selling author, high impact teacher, and former senator, Dr. Trimm is a sought-after empowerment specialist, revolutionary thinker, and transformational leader. She has earned a distinguished reputation as a catalyst for change and voice of hope to the nations.

Listed among *Ebony* magazine's *Power 100* as the "top 100 doers and influencers in the world today," Dr. Trimm is a featured speaker on some of the world's largest platforms, a frequent guest on Christian broadcasting's most popular TV and radio shows, and continually tops the Black Christian News Network and Black Christian Book Company's National Bestsellers List.

Dr. Trimm combines her wealth of leadership expertise with her depth of spiritual understanding to reveal life-transforming messages that empower and inspire. Seasoned with humor, compassion, revelatory insight, and personal candor, Dr. Trimm opens minds and touches hearts with biblically-based principles of inner healing and personal empowerment.

Pulling on her background in government, education, psychology, and human development, Dr. Trimm translates hard-hitting spiritual insights into everyday language that empower individuals to transform their lives—helping change the path people take in search of meaning, dignity, purpose, and hope.

DR. CINDY TRIMM'S
SOUL SERIES

RECLAIM *Your Soul*

Your Journey to Personal Empowerment

CURRICULUM STUDY KITS
LEARN MORE AT SOULFASTMOVEMENT.COM

The ENTIRE *Reclaim Your Soul* PRODUCT LINE

BOOK · STUDY GUIDE · JOURNAL
DVD STUDY WITH LEADER'S GUIDE

LEARN MORE AT CINDYTRIMM.COM

  DESTINY IMAGE IS A DIVISION OF NORI MEDIA GROUP.